Heartstrings and Hellish Things

Lauren Green

BookLeaf Publishing

India | USA | UK

Presentation by *BookLeaf Publishing*

Web: www.bookleafpub.com

E-mail: info@bookleafpub.com

ISBN: 9789360944742

First edition 2024

To my partner, Rob, thank you for not moaning — well, not too much — about all the books that are taking up half of our bedroom and for having my head stuck in one most evenings. Also, to my son, Alfie, though you may often decide it's time to do a puzzle or play with Lego together as soon as you see me pick my laptop or notebook up, you bring so much happiness and never fail to put a smile on my face.

ACKNOWLEDGEMENT

A huge thank you to BookLeaf Publishing for creating #TheWriteAngle challenge. As a serial procrastinator, with pages of unfinished drafts, this challenge gave me the kick I needed to focus and find time to write without excuses.

PREFACE

This collection of poems explores the darkest corners of the minds belonging to people we meet every day. Everyone has a secret, a struggle, a demon; though they don't always come to light.

This book can be enjoyed by anyone who feels more deeply than others, has dark thoughts, or feels misunderstood. Or if you just enjoy seeing words strung together to make a thought-provoking sentence, that's fine too.

Excuse Me, While I Jet-Wash
My Brain

Regrets discolour my mind
like tea-stained splodges
smeared across my memory bank.
I wish I could erase them
so I never have to be reminded;
but even my boiling tears
can't wash them away.

Trauma is also on the canvas
of my fragile, patchwork brain.
Like lines of burning tar,
seeping across, sinking low.
Buried deep are these marks
turned crispy and solid;
I cannot pluck them out.

Anger burns throughout
another realm of my emotions.
Glowing cardinal, dotted around,
it burns every so often.
Only the sea of sadness
can cool it down briefly;
still the pattern of red remains.

However hard I've tried,
I cannot seem to scrub away
the painful colours of Autumn
living inside my brain.
Let me just remove it
and blast away the flaws.
So please excuse me,
while I jet-wash my brain.

I'd Rather Be an Oddity

In the corner I hide, shying away from the
crowd,
I ache to belong, but my nerves won't do me
proud.
They laugh and chink bottles, as their
confidence arises,
funny how fast moods change, life is full of
surprises.

Is my face that strange, to make people turn
away?
Nobody ever approaches, they just get on with
their day.
They don't know my story, nor even my name,
years I've spent an outcast, wanting someone to
blame.

Belonging in the background, dark and unseen,
I wonder if I were pretty, how things could have
been.
Would there be opportunity for friendship or
love?
Should I change myself to fit their clique like a
glove?

Their joy erupts as they begin to sway together,
I will never share that happiness, not now, not
ever.
But I'd rather be an oddity than change who I
am;
after all, who'd ever like the real me, if not even
I can?

Jealousy's Seeds

Her body is a garden of envious roots
wrapping around her hateful heart.
Jealousy swimming through her veins,
will she ever repot, enjoy a fresh start?

Her poison spits wherever she speaks,
green-eyed, with a thorn for a tongue.
Once blooming, now left to decay,
unwilling to accept, she's no longer young.

Pink as a peony, once were her cheeks,
now sharp and pale, haunting to see.
She can't be forgiven for her terrible deeds.
You see, he couldn't move on from her infidelity.

Now it's her who suffers, alone and rotting.
The world has moved on, as lines have formed,
her body sags, but she won't break from plotting,
looking for revenge, for being left unforgiven.

The years go by, and alone she remains
as nothing becomes of her plate of bitterness.
She wakes, she hates, she feels, she strains,
slowly she starts to disintegrate.

So beware the swift flower of jealousy's seeds.
Amend your wrongs or you'll wither away
like an unloved plant, a mere weed;
a forgotten cluster of shrivelled leaves you'll be.

Sunflowers

Colour my arms in hues of purple,
as you grip me tightly,
painting rings and circles,
to show how much you need me.

Dot my thighs with green,
from taking the strain,
of how much you love me,
while we Iie in our marital bed.

Make my veins glow blue,
to help my mind fade away,
with the drug pumped through,
to help me be your muse.

As the colours fade,
turning yellow like sunflowers,
what a beautiful display;
shame it kills me, to be yours.

Scroll Until We're Sad

Swipe, swipe, up and down
until my thumb is aching.
Crack my fingers, stretch my neck,
God, my heart is breaking.

Double tap, leave a heart,
now comment something nice;
'OMG, I love your look',
Fuck, I hate my life.

Addicted to the scroll,
I hunt for more perfection.
Stunning homes, flawless skin,
avoiding my reflection.

Round and round I go again
as the hours pass me by.
Until I'm summoned to reality
with a desperate urge to cry.

Getting lost in endless screen time
leaves us feeling pretty bad.
So tell me, why is it that we
always scroll until we're sad?

Before You Go

Move on they say,
you'll be over him before you know it.
Yet, I can't stomach the thought
of living my days without you,
knowing of your existence elsewhere.
So, how do I learn to unlove,
to forget what we had?
Where does the journey of grieving us begin?
For so long, it's been you and I,
and it's a struggle to let that go,
when I'm unsure what being just I means.
I need to find myself once again,
go back to the child version of me,
rebuild and learn from the beginning.
But before you go, please tell me
how to cope with the grief
without a body to bury;
only the memories of our life
once packed with happiness,
now tainted with illusory.

Fuzzy Grey Lines

In his eyes, fuzzy, grey lines swim
as a static buzz is born in his ears.
His fingers tingle and slowly lose
feeling. The lines blur into a
choppy sea.
He gasps for air as he's pulled
under. A hand reaches out
but it's not to save him;
it pushes him deeper, deeper.
Black as the night, is the water
he struggles in.
His head bobs above
while creatures swim beneath.
He fights, kicks, thrashes.
Out of the water he crawls,
shivering and lost.
Returning to the moment
where words hang in the air,
that he's not sure how to process.
His emotions lack the energy
to come out and engage.
So he sits and waits
as the fuzzy grey lines
return again.

Jar Full of Clouds

People always ask
how I've been,
what I've been up to,
but I never have an answer;
because it quite often seems,
though I have plans scattered here and there,
the time in between I am simply existing,
not doing anything worth telling.
My head is a jar full of clouds,
floating with thoughts
that have no reason behind them.
Some are dark and take a while to pass,
and sometimes it rains and things get too much;
So I hide away until the pouring stops,
then I go back to the comfort of the clouds
and I'm content with just being.

Comparison Carousel

She spends her evenings sitting in the dark,
weighed down by a blanket that's seen cleaner
days.
Crumbs and confectionery wrappers
scattered everywhere in sight.
The light from her phone screen
highlights her puffy eyes
and chapped, bleeding lips.
Checking her photos in search of new likes,
feeling worthless, when no attention is shown.
Dropping emojis on snaps of people she
despises,
searching for hashtags to make her seen.
Her digital world is a curated show
of edited selfies, just like hers.
And those behind the curtains,
sit at home alone, under a blanket,
looking at others just like her;
yet no one shows the true reality
of their lonely life, so round and
round again the comparison carousel goes.

Smoky Kiss Goodbye

We need to talk, he says, as he gestures to the
chair,
my senses prickle chillingly, then silence fills
the air.
The walls fade away, as a dark cage descends,
ten years of marriage have come to an end.

My mind is trapped in a pit of darkness and
grief,
could I have done more? No, not to my belief.
Memories replay, as my heart begins to bleed,
oh so numb, this moment, I'd never have
believed.

Inside my head, a ball of fire eats away.
I'll make him sorry, for being led so easily
astray.
I pour a bottle across the room as he pauses at
the door,
I smile at him, strike a match, and drop it to the
floor.

Pieces of our life together, burn and turn to
ashes,

I raise the bottle above his head and watch as it
smashes.
Blood spills out and down he goes, unconscious
on the floor,
after a smoky kiss goodbye, I then slip out
through the door.

What a shame it is, that things turned out this
way,
but he destroyed my trust, my world, he simply
had to pay.

Intrusive Thoughts

15

Swing swing
back and forth
she doesn't care
my thoughts go.

It's all an act
she's not your friend
can't you see
it's all pretend.

She's using you
to fill the time
there's no interest
in your life.

Laughter echoes
behind your back
red nose drawn
gossip spreads.

You're just a doll
left in a box
forgotten about
until she's bored.

But cheers girl
clink clink
raise a toast
to friendship.

Stuck in the Slow Lane of Life

Everyone is moving forward but me.
Years I've spent dreaming of bigger things,
working relentlessly to feel free.
A belt with skills stuffed tightly underneath,
yet I'm still not where I thought I'd be.

How is it that those the same age as me,
have a marriage, a house, a family?
While I'm still living as a child,
my worries and fears ever-growing,
I remain meek and mild.

Stuck in a job that makes me unhappy,
and though I don't have many bills to pay,
I don't find it hard to squander money away.
Takeaways, or new clothes, I don't try to save;
I'm not moving forward, so like a child I behave.

However hard I've tried, to find my dream job
or a connection with a love interest,
nothing ends well. Maybe I need a therapist.
Will I ever have a family of my own?
A job that I'm proud of, or buy my own home?

Only time will tell I suppose,
I'm used to being stuck in the slow lane
of life, and I've only myself to blame.
As we are all in control of our own destiny,
maybe it's time to push myself into the fast lane.

Apple Core

There's a woman across the road, who everyone
avoids.
She never has a nice word to say about anyone,
sticking her nose in every scenario, always
paranoid.
Thinking she's the topic of the world's
discussion,
her likeability has been completely destroyed.

Believing she's above everyone, though it's not
clear why.
No friends have stuck around, and family
despise her,
people used to make an effort, now no one wants
to try.
She treats kindness as a weakness and won't help
a soul,
she'll laugh in the face of anyone who dares to
cry.

Those once in her life did nothing but give,
she didn't appreciate anyone around her.
Whenever confronted, she went on the
defensive;
but illness has caused her to question her choices

now she's older and doesn't have much longer to
live.

That's why it's important, to be nice you see,
otherwise, you'll be forgotten, unthought of
like fruit, discarded to the planet's needs.
Rotting away by yourself, with no one to care,
an apple core left, sad and bitter you'll be.

Injured Blackbird

A blackbird with an injured wing
rests against a wooden gate.
The gate belongs to a cottage,
where the shell of a woman lives.
She sits all day, looking out at the world
unable to speak, or feel anything.
As large as a mansion, is her shattered mind,
left to gather dust, no new memories to fill the
rooms.
The light has gone out, the corridors dark.
The years have taught her so much,
but the trauma she's endured
has pushed the books she once stored
on the shelves of her mind, into the abyss.
What a shame for the pages once turned
and learned to be forgotten, erased.
Locked away are the words, and snippets of her
life,
unable to access without the key,
buried under years of psychological torture,
too deep to dig up, too painful to try.
So all she can do is sit by the window,
and look out at the gate
where the injured blackbird sits,
hurting just as much as she is.

The Pain That Festers

Why do we find it hard to forgive ourselves
for a mistake we made in a different decade?
When we were someone else entirely,
with the whole world yet to learn,
unknowing that just one bad move
would cause our minds an eternal burn.

Yet, we forgive other people
who have also done us wrong,
as it's easier living with external wounds
then the pain that festers inside of us.
So we punish ourselves for eternity,
reliving our mistakes.
Angry that we're the ones,
who caused our fragile hearts
to break.

My Demons Dance With Me

So, so tired is my heated mind,
barely able to get through the day,
unable to focus on anything in
the light.

It's only when there's darkness
that I feel my mind switch on;
exhausted from pretending
its limits go beyond.

Sleep calls and I stand alone
in a ballroom, dark and eerie,
feeling the arms of my demons
envelop and protect me.

A comforting embrace as
they grin and hold me tight,
we share secrets silently and
dance through the night.

Every turn and step makes
me feel like I belong;
normally so cold inside, now
I feel my soul gently burn.

They take it in turns to hold
my hand, claws piercing skin;
I let them even though it means
I'll be damned for eternity.

When the sky is full of light
I have no friends to see,
but at least in the darkness
my demons dance with me.

Girl Through the Glass

Through the glass beside me,
her eyes catch mine.
Brown as the leaves
that crunch under my boots.
Drooping with the weight
of the burdens she carries;
not just her own, but those belonging to others.
You can tell by the way her shoulders slump,
checking her phone in an anxious state,
as if she needed to process
whatever it shows without delay.
Desperate for someone to shoulder the brunt
of her unsolvable difficulties.
To take a stone away, even a pebble or two,
anything to lighten the heaviness
that's dragging her down.
If only I could reach across,
place my hand on her shoulder,
and tell her that one day
she'll have time to breathe again.
But I can't see brighter days ahead,
and it would hurt her more
to give false hope, of a calmer future
that I'm not sure exists.
I know this, because the girl through the glass,
well, of course, she is me.

Lost in Thought

'Are you okay?' he asked, as her eyes brimmed
silently.
Behind her calm exterior, her mind was battling.
A storm raged within her thoughts, worries
flying free,
of things that hadn't happened yet but brewed
quietly.

Anxieties whisper in her ear, all hours of the day,
she thinks they are protecting her, so she lets
them out to play.
If only she had the strength, to silence them for
good,
she'd be able to talk freely without being
misunderstood.

Lightning strikes and hits a nerve, as the storm
begins to swirl,
overwhelmed with her emotions, her head
begins to twirl.
The storm passes after a while and her body
starts to rest,
'I'm fine', she says, 'just lost in thought', feelings
now recessed.

The Quiet Ones

27

Those who think you are quiet,
are yet to see the darkness that wears your soul.
Kept hidden inside,
thoughts that would disturb anyone who cared;
but they don't ask, so you don't tell.
Urges to cause suffering to the body you belong
to,
because it's the only thing that makes you feel
something.
So the quiet ones really can be quite terrifying.

A Simple Puppet

I stand in the crowded theatre of life,
a simple puppet, wearing many masks.
The strings are long and twisted,
limbs ready to be bent, manipulated.

A life that follows the script of others,
written by people that I'm a stranger to.
Twists at the end of every chapter,
always morphing into a new character.

No face stares back at me in the mirror,
a void within myself, skin and bones alone.
Expressions change with each new scene,
none of them showing what's within.

Borrowed lines, emotions rehearsed,
body becoming stiffer with each new show.
Limp and tired, my mind rests, while
my strings are tugged by the puppeteer.

So who am I, in this production?
An empty fool, there to entertain,
longing to find my identity, and
hoping that one day the strings will fray.

Particle of Dust

'It's not good news', the doctor says.
And as he talks, my mind detaches
from my body. And drifts away
towards the window, open just a crack.
Up and out I go, like a particle of dust
floating higher. Ah. this is nice,
I can't feel anything.
I'm in the air, amongst other specks
that have been swept away
from the surface.
I pass others, with a similar destiny,
this isn't so bad I suppose.
I'll stay here until reality comes calling
and I need a surface to rest on.
Though I'm simply another particle
of dust swept away, at least for now
I am free.

www.ingramcontent.com/pod-product-compliance
Lightning Source LLC
LaVergne TN
LVHW010838200726
843508LV00012B/2656